Engineering construction risks

An SERC project report

Engineering construction risks

a guide to project risk analysis and assessment

implications for project clients and project managers

Edited by P. A. Thompson and J. G. Perry

 Thomas Telford, London

Report of research supported by the Science and Engineering Research Council and prepared by the Project Management Group, the University of Manchester Institute of Science and Technology, and the School of Civil Engineering, University of Birmingham

Published by Thomas Telford Services Ltd, Thomas Telford House, 1 Heron Quay, London E14 4JD

First published 1986 under the title *Risk management in engineering construction*

This edition published 1992

A catalogue record for this book is available from the British Library

ISBN: 0 7277 1665 4

Typeset in Great Britain by Ashford Overload

Printed and bound in Great Britain by Eastern Press Ltd.

Contents

Introduction and conclusions

All human endeavour involves risk. The success or failure of any venture depends on how we deal with it. The construction industry has had a poor reputation for coping with risk, many projects failing to meet deadlines and cost targets. Clients, contractors, the public and others have suffered as a result.

This report is the result of studies with the industry on how risk analysis and risk management may be used to improve the financial success of engineering construction projects. The work was supported by the Science and Engineering Research Council, in two stages. The first stage ran for three years, from 1983 to 1986; its results were summarised in our report *Risk Management in Engineering Construction* produced for the SERC in 1986 and distributed by Thomas Telford Ltd. The second stage ran for two years, 1990-1991. The results of both stages are summarised in this revised and expanded report. The authors are the research team listed in appendix C.

The report spells out the importance of tackling the risks of projects, and shows how this can be done. It also provides an introduction to the literature on the subject. Its aim is to increase awareness of this vital issue among the industry and its clients, in both the public and private sectors. Its principal conclusions are as follows.

- **All too often risk is either ignored or dealt with in an arbitrary way:** simply adding a 10% 'contingency' onto the estimated cost of a project is typical. This is virtually certain to be inadequate and cause expensive delay, litigation, and perhaps bankruptcy (see chapters 1 and 4).
- The greatest uncertainty is in the **earliest stages** of a project, which is also when decisions of greatest impact are made. Risk must be assessed and allowed for at this stage (chapter 2).
- The client's departments and advisers should operate as a single team to avoid the **institutional risk** of incomplete commitment and inconsistent decisions (chapter 2).
- **Flexibility in project design** and the **risk of later changes** should be considered in detail before completing proposals for sanctioning (chapter 2).
- Risks change during most projects. Risk management should therefore be a **continuing activity** throughout the life of a project (chapter 2).

- Much can be learned about the implications and management of project risk without extensive numerical analysis. Risk analysis is essentially a brain-storming process of compiling **realistic forecasts and answers to 'what happens if ?' questions** (chapter 1).

- The quantitative techniques can be used to analyse probabilities and the sensitivity of predictions to uncertainties in estimates to give **a much more accurate assessment** of risks (chapter 3 and case study in appendix A).

- Risk techniques are widely used in other industries. **The techniques are now well within the reach of small companies,** requiring only a microcomputer to be put into action.

- The assessment of risk requires analysis of the likely extent and interaction of variable factors. The analysis should be carried out by those trained to do so jointly with project planners and cost estimators. **The need for judgement should not be used as an excuse for failing to give adequate consideration to project or contract risk.**

- On most construction projects, the client deceives himself if he uses single figure estimates of cost and time for appraisal and funding decisions. **Ranges of estimates should be used,** including **specific contingencies** and **tolerances** for uncertainty (chapter 4).

- **Delay** in completion can be the greatest cause of extra cost, and of loss of financial return and other benefits from a project. **The first estimate of cost and benefits should be based on a realistic programme** for a project. On this basis the potential effects of delays can be predicted realistically (chapter 4).

- Attention to contract strategy based upon systematic consideration of risk can achieve significant cost savings for a project. There is growing acceptance in the UK that traditional contractual arrangements are no longer the best basis for managing today's high-risk projects. **The proposals for funding (sanction) a project should therefore include recommendations on contract strategy** (chapter 5).

- **Competitive tendering** coupled with **traditional contractual arrangements** limit the realistic management of risk. The pressure is always on those bidding for contracts to keep their tender prices as low as possible, which can put both them and their clients at great financial risk if things go wrong. When some provision has been made for eventualities, it is often buried in the total bid. This hinders the effective management of risk and militates against a systematic and equitable basis of payments (chapters 6 and 7).

- For high-risk contracts, project sponsors should **specify the allocation of risk** when inviting bids and require tenderers to **state their provision for risk** in their bids (chapter 6). Project sponsors should also consider **selecting the contractor on the basis of 'minimum acceptable risk' rather than lowest price.** Risk analysis allows such a criterion to be used (chapter 7).

- **Joint ventures** and consortia are means of sharing resources and risks, but should be based on **partnership and commitment** (chapter 2).

- **Public authorities** should review the **cost-effectiveness** of their policies and procedures for dealing with risk. **Project managers should be given the authority to manage project risks, and restrictions on the choice of contract arrangements and tendering procedures should be removed** where they lead to inefficiency.

- The overriding conclusion drawn from the research is that clients and all parties involved in construction projects and contracts benefit greatly from **reduction in uncertainty prior to their financial commitment.** Money spent early buys more than money spent late. Willingness to invest in anticipating risk is a test of a client's wish for a successful project.

The study draws on collaborative work with companies and public authorities for projects in the UK and overseas. References are given to more detailed publications and case studies.

Definitions

The following definitions are used in this report.

Client - meaning also 'promoter', 'employer', 'principal', 'owner' or 'purchaser', as used in various sets of model conditions of contract.

Project - a new structure, system or service and also a substantial renovation, extension or replacement.

Sanction - the decision to authorize investment in a project.

Tender - meaning also a 'bid' or any offer to enter into a contract.

Variation - a change to a contractor's work ordered under a term of contract (the 'variations clause').

Facility - the structure or system resulting from a project.

Risk analysis and management - an overview

Risk and uncertainty are inherent in all construction work no matter what the size of a project. Size can be one of the major causes of risk, so can changes in political or commercial planning. Other factors carrying risk with them include the complexity of the project, location, speed of construction and familiarity with the type of work. Road and reservoir maintenance work and most building refurbishment are examples of smaller but risky projects.

The evidence of many projects in this country and overseas reveals that these risks are not being adequately dealt with. Figs 1 and 2 shows the extent of cost and time overruns of projects financed by the World Bank reviewed between 1974 and 1988 [1]. In the UK, a 1975 report on the performance of public sector construction projects found that one in six contracts overran by more than 40% of the original contract period, and a significant number by more than 80%

1.1 Project risks

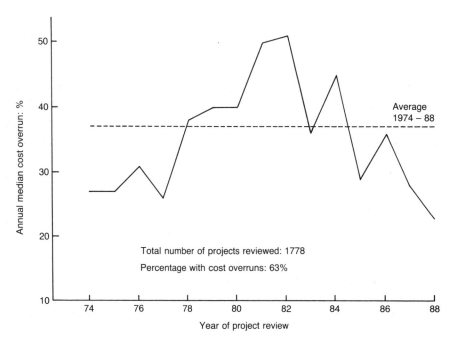

Fig. 1. Overrun of actual costs of projects compared with cost estimated at time of appraisal. Some of the more recent decline in cost overruns is attributed to a greater amount of design being completed before project sanctioning, and some to more systematic use of contingencies, but another factor was that many projects were reduced in scope after sanctioning

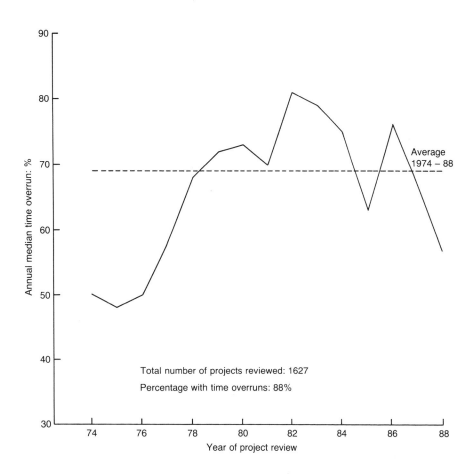

Fig. 2. Overrun of project completion times

5

[2]. A 1983 study on the speed of industrial building in the UK [3] confirmed that too many projects overrun both cost and time targets and, significantly, it found definite evidence that greater attention to project management produced significant improvement in meeting targets.

Time and cost overruns can invalidate the economic case for a project, turning a potentially profitable investment into a loss-maker. Fig. 3 shows that this occurred on a significant number of projects reviewed earlier by the World Bank [4].

Targets are sometimes missed because of unforeseen events that even an experienced project manager cannot anticipate. More often it happens because of events that are predictable in general, but not in specific terms. For example, industrial disputes, delayed decisions or unexpected ground conditions may all be anticipated, but their likelihood and impact are hard to predict with any precision, as no two construction projects are the same. This makes it important to identify the sources of risk for each project.

It is useful to group risks according to simple measures of their probability and likely impact. Not all will be possible calamities. Costs may be less than anticipated, the weather may be kind, revenues may exceed expectation. Risk can sometimes be beneficial, and this must also be taken into account.

Figure 3 also shows a small proportion of projects where the overall impact of risk was highly beneficial to the project economics. This should not lead to

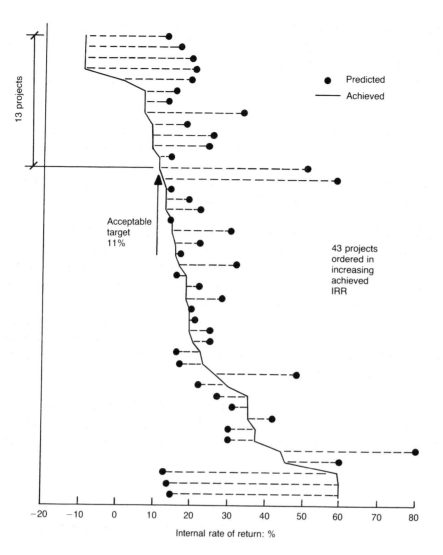

Fig. 3. Development projects: predicted compared with achieved internal rate of return

complacency, as inaccurate predictions always lead to inefficient use of resources. The message of Fig. 3 and the other reports cited is that risk needs to be better understood, through risk analysis, and better controlled, through risk management.

In project management terms the most serious *effects* of risk can be summarised as follows:

- failure to keep within the cost estimate
- failure to achieve the required completion date
- failure to achieve the required quality and operational requirements.

The purpose of risk analysis and management is to help managers avoid these failures.

Risk analysis and management are not easy. They are better done systematically in stages.

The previous version of this report drew on a terminology for three stages proposed by Healy [5], among others. Our further research, close collaboration with the Specific Interest Group on Risk of the Association of Project Managers [6], and the work of the Construction Industry Institute in the USA [7,8] show that different terminologies and perceptions of content exist among experienced

1.2 Systematic risk analysis and risk management

risk analysts and managers. Differences in perceptions can be subtle, and so the research team has used a simple model of the stages of risk analysis and management. This model is effective, and has proved acceptable to a wide range of experienced practitioners. In it the process is divided into risk analysis and risk management.

Risk analysis can be qualitative and quantitative. Firstly the sources of risk must be identified. Secondly their effects must be assessed or analysed.

Risk management requires management responses and policies to reduce and control the main risks identified in the analysis.

Risk analysis and management are not intended to kill off worthwhile projects, nor to dampen levels of capital investment. The aims are, firstly, to ensure that only those projects which are genuinely worthwhile are sanctioned and, secondly, to avoid excessive overruns. When applying the techniques, attitude of mind is important, and we emphasise that it should be viewed as a constructive process. Risk analysis and management can be the most creative tasks of project management. They should generate realism, and so increase a commitment to control. Through encouraging problem-solving, they open the way to innovative solutions to getting a project completed.

The burden of responsibility for identifying risks and dealing with them rests with the client and his project manager [9,10]. The threat posed to the success of the project should provide reason enough to take the ideas behind risk analysis and management seriously.

1.3 Qualitative risk analysis

This process has two aims: risk identification ; and initial risk assessment.

The objective is to compile a list of the main risk sources and a description of their likely consequences, perhaps including a first approximation of their potential effect on estimates of cost and time [11]. Research has shown that a practicable target is to compile a list of between 5 and 10 main risks for a project - or for each work package if the project is large or complex. Three techniques are commonly used

- check lists of risk compiled from previous experience
- interviews with key project participants
- brain-storming with the project team

Many managers believe that this initial qualitative analysis is essential and that it brings considerable benefits in terms of understanding the project and its potential problems, as well as provoking thought about the management responses to the risks. The research has observed some cases where a project has been totally re-thought as a result of this analysis.

The realism of estimates increases as a project proceeds, but, of course, the most influential decisions are made early in the life of projects. So, despite the difficulties, a realistic estimate of the final cost and duration of the total project is required as early as possible. It is then that all the potential risk and uncertainties which can affect these estimates and act as constraints on the project should be identified.

There is a second, equally important, reason for the early identification of risk and uncertainty: it should focus the attention of senior managers on the need for strategies for the control and allocation of risk, for example through the choice of a contract strategy. It will also make obvious what further design, development work or other actions, such as clarifying objectives, is most needed.

1.4 Quantitative risk analysis

Quantitative analysis usually involves more sophisticated analysis techniques, often requiring computer programs. To some people this is the most formal aspect of the whole process, requiring

- estimates of uncertainty in predicting the cost and duration of activities
- probabilistic combination of individual uncertainties.

Chapter 3 of this report and the case study in appendix A describe some of these techniques. Such techniques can be applied with varying levels of effort and resources, ranging from a few days using relatively simple programs, to several man-months using different programs.

Mathematical models and analytical techniques can be useful indicators of trends and problems for attention; they should not be relied on as the sole guide to decisions. Their accuracy depends on the realism of assumptions made, the skill of the model builder and the accuracy of the data used.

We recommend that companies new to risk analysis and management start slowly, perhaps ignoring quantitative analysis, until confidence is gained. Analysis can then be extended to judging the probability of occurrence of each risk and its possible consequences. An example is the project sanction decision for clients where estimates of cost and time can be produced in the form of ranges and associated probabilities, rather than the traditional single figure values. The collective effect of many risks is to delay construction and commissioning, both of which can increase the final cost and also reduce the financial return expected from a project. The quantitative techniques available can be used to estimate the potential cost of such delays and thus help produce a realistic cost-benefit analysis and budget.

A company's procedures for decision-making may need to be modified to make good use of quantitative risk analysis. Experience has shown that using qualitative analysis quickly leads to some quantitative analysis, and the pressure for more rigorous analysis can quickly build up.

1.5 Risk management

This part of the process involves the formulation of management responses to the main risks. It may start during the qualitative analysis phase, as the need to respond to some risks may be urgent and the solution fairly obvious. Interaction between the risk analysis and management phases is common.

The greater the uncertainties the more flexible the response must be. In the extreme, risks may have such serious consequences as to demand a reappraisal of a project or even its complete abandonment. It is more likely that risk identification and analysis will reveal a need for re-design, more detailed design, further site investigation, a different packaging of the work content, the use of alternative contract strategies or different methods of construction.

8

Risk management can involve

- identifying preventive measures to avoid a risk or to reduce its effects
- proceeding with a project stage-by-stage, initiating further investigation to reduce uncertainty through better information [9]
- considering risk transfer in contract strategy, with attention to the motivational effects and the control of risk allocation
- considering risk transfer to insurers
- setting and managing risk allowances in cost estimates, programmes and specifications
- establishing contingency plans to deal with risks if they occur.

Risk management will not *remove* all risk from projects; its principal aim is to ensure that risks are *managed most efficiently*. The client and his project manager must recognise that certain risks will remain to be carried by the client. This 'residual risk' must be allowed for in the client's estimate of time and cost.

Effective management of risky projects demands rapid and realistic predictions of alternative courses of action and positive decision-making. It requires flexible attitudes and procedures; however institutional constraints frequently conflict with these requirements. Despite its clear importance, risk analysis is not yet widely used on construction projects in the public sector, though it is frequently applied to private sector projects. The public sector should follow their example. There is an urgent need for politicians and their advisors, as well as those involved in construction projects, to examine current procedures used in the planning and implementation of projects, because some of these are causing unnecessary delay, avoidable costs and poor performance.

If risks can be transferred or re-allocated, their consequences will be shared with, or totally carried by, someone other than the client [12,13]. The client should expect to pay a premium for this, so responsibility for adopting this risk response must therefore lie with the client, who should ensure it is in his own best interest to transfer the risk. Again, this will demand careful analysis of both his own and the other parties' objectives, the relative abilities of the parties to assume the risk, and the degree of control over the situation.

Clearly, risk management has major benefits for any enterprise. It is more than just a way of helping to get projects completed on time and to budget. For example, it can

- enable decision-making to be more systematic and less subjective
- allow comparison of the robustness of projects to specific uncertainties
- make the relative importance of each risk immediately apparent
- give an improved understanding of the project through identifying the risks and thinking through response scenarios
- demonstrate company responsibility to customers
- have a powerful impact on management by forcing a realisation that there is a range of possible outcomes for a project
- improve corporate experience and communication.

9

1. World Bank. *Annual review of project performance results*. Operations Evaluation Department, World Bank, 1990.

2. NEDO. *The public client and the construction industries*. 1975.

3. NEDO. *Faster building for industry*. 1983.

4. Independent Group on Real Aid. *Real aid: a strategy for Britain*. Oxford University Press, 1982, extracted from Sixth annual review, World Bank, 1980.

5. N. J. Healy. *Risk management in giant civil engineering projects*. University of Manchester (UMIST), MSc thesis, 1981.

6. C. Norris et al. *A guide to project risk analysis and management*. Specific Interest Group, Association of Project Managers (pull-out in *Project*, Apr. 1992).

7. J. E. Diekmann *et al. Risk management in capital projects*. Construction Industry Institute, Texas, 1988, Source document 41.2.

8. D. B. Ashley *et al. Impact of risk allocation and equity in construction contracts*. Construction Industry Institute, Texas, 1989, Source document 44.

9. R. Youker. Managing the project cycle for time, cost and quality: lessons from World Bank experience. *Int. J. Project Manage.*, 1989, **7**, 52-57.

10. P. A. Thompson. The client role in project management. *Int. J. Project Manage.*, 1991, **9**, 90-92.

11. J. G. Perry. Risk management - an approach for project managers. *Int. J. Project Manage.*, 1980, **4**, 211-216.

12. S. C. Ward and C. B. Chapman. Extending the use of risk analysis in project management. *Int. J. Project Manage.*, 1991, **9**, 117-123.

13. S. C. Ward *et al*. On the allocation of risk in construction projects. *Int. J. Project Manage.*, 1991, **9**, 140-147.

References

10

2 When to apply risk management

Risk management is most valuable early in a project proposal, while there is still the flexibility in design and planning to consider how the serious risks may be avoided. Not all can be avoided, for instance changes in the predictions of the demand for the service or product, and the risks can change. Risk management should, therefore, be continued throughout the life of a project. It should influence each stage of commitment by the client, especially these three stages, which are shown in Fig 4:

- in deciding the project 'master plan' or brief resulting from the evaluation of various schemes in the project appraisal stage;
- in preparing the final proposal for sanction (funding);
- in deciding the contract strategy and basis for awarding contracts;

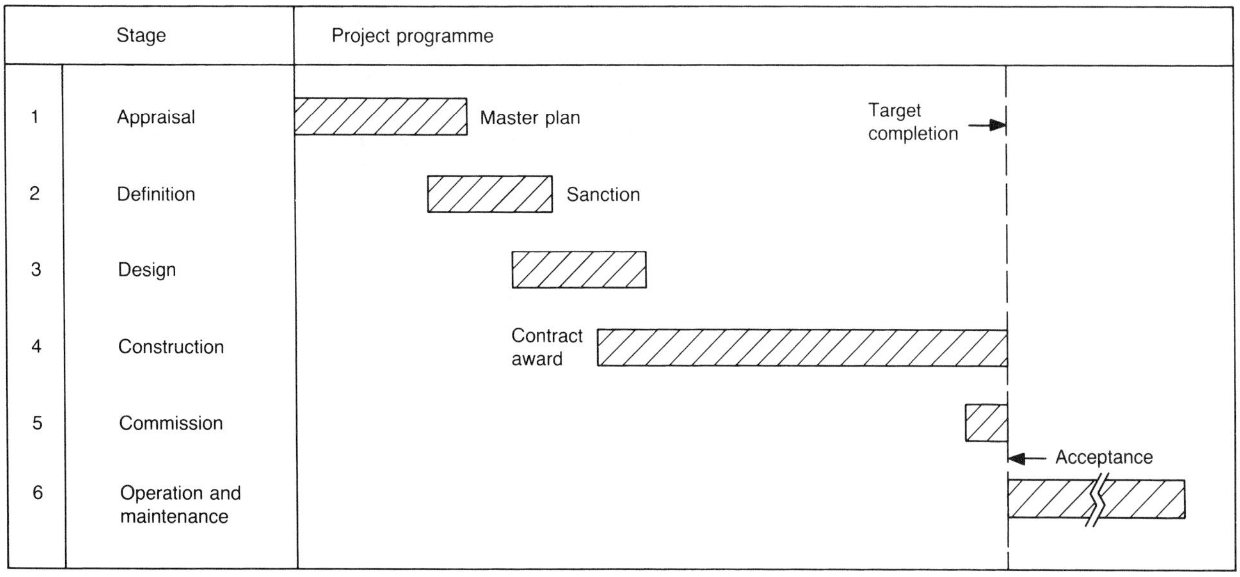

Fig. 4. Main stages of a project. The time required to appraise proposals and define a project for sanctioning can vary from a matter of days for emergency projects, to many years for complex or politically sensitive projects such as a nuclear power scheme or a tidal barrage. One to three years is typical of the duration of construction projects from sanction to acceptance by the users. Some risky and quite expensive project work can be much shorter, for instance a motorway maintenance contract

	Stage	Project programme
1	Appraisal	Master plan ... Target completion
2	Definition	Sanction
3	Design	
4	Construction	Contract award
5	Commission	
6	Operation and maintenance	Acceptance

As pointed out above, the greatest uncertainty is encountered early in the life of a new project. Consequently, decisions taken during the earliest stages of a project can have a very large impact on its final cost and its duration. Change is an unavoidable feature of many projects, but its likely extent and effects are frequently under-estimated during these early phases.

Applying risk management at the project appraisal stage will give the client a much clearer idea of the project, and will enable decisions to be made with far more confidence.

What are the major sources of risk in project appraisal ? Table 1 gives a list of risks which have been found to be important. Project managers are recommended to develop their own detailed lists based on their experience and the type of project, as for instance have Perry and Hayes [14] for civil engineering work.

These risks can affect the estimates of project cost and the predictions of cash flows needed in project appraisal to make decisions between alternative schemes, test their economic justification and assess the financing needed. The analysis of the risks should

- provide the basis for setting realistic contingencies and estimating tolerances consistent with the objective of preparing the best estimate of anticipated total project cost
- indicate comparative differences in the riskiness of alternative project schemes.

Resources are not usually expended in defining a project in detail before appraisal has shown whether it is worth proceeding with. Appraisal therefore cannot be accurate. We recommend that effort at this stage should be concentrated on

- seeking solutions which avoid or at least reduce risk
- considering whether the extents or natures of the major risks are such that the normal ways of transferring the risk to other parties may be impossible or particularly expensive

2.1 Risk in project appraisal

Table 1. *Sources of risk*

Source	Example
Client, Government, regulatory agencies	Bureaucratic delays, changes in local regulations
Funding, fiscal	Changes in Government funding policy, liaison between several funders
Definition of project	Change in project scope
Project organisation	Authority of project manager, involvement of outside bodies
Design	Adequacy to meet need, realism of design programme
Local conditions	Local customs, weather windows
Permanent plant supply	Degree of novelty, damage or loss during transportation
Construction contractors	Experience, financial stability
Construction materials	Excessive wastage, quality, delivery
Construction labour	Industrial relations, multi-racial labour force
Construction plant	Resale value, spares availability
Logistics	Remoteness, access to site
Estimating data	Relevance to specific project, availability
Inflation	
Exchange rates	
Force majeure	

- outlining any special strategies for risk transfer, for instance by insurance or unconventional contractual arrangements.

2.2 Risk in funding decisions

This stage, commonly known as 'sanction' by clients, is of critical importance in the life of a project, as it leads to the major expenditure on design, procurement, and construction.

Traditionally, a sanction proposal includes a cost estimate, project programme, and technical specification. The cost estimate and programme should allow for risk, as discussed in chapter 4. There should also be an extra component in the proposal - namely a plan for risk management which will concentrate on contract strategy but may include other proposals such as insurance. The choice of contract strategy should be based on consideration of the responsibilities for the risks of design, construction and services, their interfaces, the division of work packages, the number and type of contracts, and methods of selecting the contractor.

2.3 Risk in contracts

Risk cannot be eliminated through the drafting and placing of contracts, but the strategy chosen or assumed for dealing with risk in contracts can greatly influence how risks are managed. The contractual arrangements and terms have a significant influence on the risk carried by each party and on the clarity with which they are perceived, and therefore on the cost, quality and duration of the project.

The main decisions where the client can gain from risk management are

- in formulating contract terms, particularly in choosing an equitable risk allocation
- in assessing the opportunities for risk management made possible by different types of contractual arrangements
- in choosing terms ('conditions') of contract which define the risks and their allocation and provide incentives for the efficient management of risks as they occur during construction.

These are covered in more detail in chapters 5 and 6.

Before tenders are invited the client or his advisers should prepare an up-to-date estimate of the expected tender price based on the information contained in the tender documents. This should be used to

- assess the consequences of risk allocation
- check the adequacy of the information in the documents
- provide a criterion for assessing contractors' tenders, particularly in judging how risks will affect the relationship between final contract price and tender amount, and between final completion date and the tendered programme;
- strengthen the client's position in contract negotiation and in subsequent contract management.

Risks in the evaluation of tenders are discussed in chapter 7.

Among the client's staff and advisers some, if not all, of the risks relevant to a project are usually known, but each risk may be known to only some of them. If recognised, a risk also tends to be seen differently by engineering, financial, commercial and legal departments, by the eventual users of the completed facility, and by general managers and their advisers [9,15]. The attitudes, experience and careers of individuals may cause genuine differences of understanding of objectives, and so affect their evaluations and perceptions of risk. Differences can be particularly acute between client, consultants, bankers and insurers on export projects. These 'institutional' risks can seriously affect the initial identification and subsequent management of potential risks crucial to project success.

The remedy is the familiar recommendation to develop 'team work' to obtain and apply the experience of users, all levels of staff and outsiders. The value of doing so is commonly acknowledged by managers, but not so often achieved. What it demands is bringing people together, and maintaining this from the stage of preparing the proposals for sanction through to the handing over of the facility for operation. The most important data is likely to be known by those with recent experience of completing other projects. To draw on this requires senior managers to consult down to this level, and to do so directly in order to avoid the bureaucratic problem of intermediaries shaping information to suit what they think the seniors want to hear.

The client's institutional risks may influence all others, as it is the client who can take action to identify, anticipate and avoid their potential effects [10]. All other parties are limited by what the client agrees needs attention. Every contractor clearly should also have a co-ordinated policy on risk management [16], but unless the client recognises a risk the other parties to a project will tend to give attention to it only as far as they think wise to protect their own interests.

2.4 Institutional risk

Joint ventures and consortia (JVCs) are attractive to project clients and contractors for undertaking some projects, but also may incur risks unfamiliar to their members or to others.

Cases indicate that the reasons for entering into a JVC vary [17-19]. They include a wish to combine resources and spread the risks of a project, for instance for a BOT or BOOT contract [20]. They are most typically formed for temporary or selective co-operation, for the purpose of carrying out one project. Some are continuing arrangements for development work, a series of related projects or for the operation of completed facilities, but they are selective in that the members continue with their other business activities independently, sometimes in competition.

The special risks to the members of a JVC are in foreseeing and agreeing what relationships and commitments between them are needed to control and carry out their external commitments to others. The main risks to the client and other parties are that the internal structure does not support the completion of its external obligations. The two lessons are therefore that from the start the members of a JVC should agree on an organizational structure suitable for *completing* their intended projects, and the structure should be designed to *minimize inter-dependence* between the members.

2.5 Joint ventures and consortia

The breakdown of work for a project between members which would result from applying the above lessons may not be what one or more of them would prefer or is used to handling. This should be anticipated at the creation of a JVC, by agreeing to form a legal partnership or separate company suitable for carrying through all its commitments and discharging its liabilities. Loraine [21] gives a checklist for the terms of a joint venture agreement.

The style and system of management appropriate for co-operative concentration on one project at a time are likely to be different to the styles and systems used in the members' organizations for their normal business. A JVC is a means of spreading risk, but to do so it demands a spread of control.

Few individuals work in more than one JVC in their career and can take the experience to another, so many managers new to a JVC may not be aware of the risks. The above lessons need emphasis whenever forming a JVC is not the normal experience, role or longer-term interest of the members. The detailed lessons, organizational choices, risks and remedies are being reviewed in a separate paper resulting from the research [19].

15

2.6 Project size and design flexibility

Ideally design should be complete and final, and a plan for project execution should be agreed before the decision to sanction a project. In practice this is not achieved because of uncertainties in market, political or physical conditions. The flexibility for these uncertainties can tempt the client and engineers to make avoidable changes, particularly if using contract and internal procedures evolved to order variations.

The lessons of successful projects provide the following answers to the above [22,23].

- Consider design options before project sanctioning. Even under pressures to limit expenditure, this is the time to consider alternatives and preferences, so as to know **how** to proceed when the decision is made **whether** to go ahead with the project.
- List the acceptable reasons for later changes.
- Involve and commit all downstream parties to the above decisions, motivating them to feel that they own the project and are personally responsible for the results.
- Decide all novel and uncertain design in detail before project sanctioning, so as to have a basis for assessing the risks and also the effects of changes if proposed later.
- Plan the project execution to the same extent of detail, so as to incorporate space and other margins for construction, commissioning and operation.
- As in budgeting, match or merge margins where possible to allow for two or more accepted risks.
- After project sanctioning consider no design changes except those imposed by law or which promise at least **double** the financial rate of return or other base criterion for the sanctioning of the project.
- Maintain continuity of the senior staff, particularly those responsible for the engineering decisions.
- If the project is novel, design in stages and concentrate expenditure in the first stage on work which will reduce the uncertainties of whether and how to proceed with the project.

- If the project is urgent, make final design decisions before starting construction. Overlapping design and construction can cause greater delays than it promises to save.

Some experienced clients and engineers state that the recurrent lesson of their projects is that design should be complete and 'frozen' at the stage of approving a project. Some describe design freezing as 'essential'. Clearly it isn't essential, as many projects are achieved satisfactorily without doing so. If design is frozen in a rigid way, the concept and the phrase can mislead people on a project into thinking that they do not need to allow for irresistible forces for revision such as markets, mistakes or new data having specific effects on safety. Freezing in detail at the start is the policy to follow only if no reasons whatever will be accepted for changing decisions previously made, for instance on an emergency project where speed is the overriding basis for decisions.

2.7 Design freezing

The practical lesson of industrial and public projects is that design flexibility and spare capacity are needed because of uncertainties of project construction, operation and maintenance, but to use them successfully there must be

- a system that controls how and when they are used
- a contract strategy appropriate for the expected extent of variations.

Flexibility and spare capacity without control to discipline how they are used can become a cover for poor initial decisions.

Size is one of the most direct influences on the capital cost of a project and on its operating worth for producing goods and services. To minimise the risk of later changes or drastic rebuilding the client should give attention to **how** decisions on the size or capacity of a project are to be made, as well as their content. A range of size, capacity and margins should be and usually is considered. The detailed implications of size should be studied before project sanctioning. Design work itself is relatively cheap, so that attention to detail can cost much less than it saves by avoiding later problems, delays or rework.

References

14. J. G. Perry and R. W. Hayes. Construction projects - know the risks. *Chartered Mech. Engr*, 1985, Feb., 42-45.

15. S. H. Wearne. Institutional risks in project management. To be published.

16. J. Al-Bahar and B. C. Gerwick. Setting up a risk management policy in contracting firms. *Proc. Project Management Institute symposium*. Calgary, 1990, 702-707.

17. J. A. Armitt. Joint ventures, formation and operation. *Management of International Projects conference*. ICE, London, 1985.

18. J. F. McFadzean. Crossing the Conway. *Project*, 1990, June.

19. S. H. Wearne and D. Wright. Joint ventures and consortia organization risks. To be published.

20. D. G. Woodward *et al*. BOOT contracts. *Project*, 1991, Apr., 28-30.

21. R. K. Loraine. *Construction management in developing countries*. Thomas Telford, London, 1991.

22. R. Gaisford. Project management in the North Sea. *Int. J. Project Manage.*, 1986, **4**, Feb., 5-13.

23. S. H. Wearne. Project design flexibility. *Engng Manage. J.*, 1992, October.

3 Quantitative techniques for project risk analysis

3.1 Introduction

A simple method for considering project risks would be to analyze any risk independently of others, with no attempt to estimate the probability of occurrence of that risk. The estimated effects of each risk could then be accumulated to provide maximum and minimum project outcome values.

Though more complex, greater realism and confidence can be achieved by applying probabilities to the risks and considering the inter-dependencies between the risks. The two most useful techniques for doing so are **sensitivity analysis** and **probability analysis,** as discussed in this chapter.

The choice of risk analysis technique to be used should depend upon many factors, principally

- the type and size of project
- the information available
- the cost of the analysis and the time available to carry it out
- the experience and expertise of the analysts.

3.2 Use of computers

The application of any risk analysis technique requires that the uncertain data can be given a range of different values. For example, if the duration and costs for specific activities are uncertain, use a range of values within which the decision maker believes they are likely to lie.

Most quantitative risk analysis techniques therefore require the speed and processing power of a computer. There are now computer programs available which are designed to carry out risk analyses and many of these programs can be adapted to the needs of individual clients and organizations.

A joint university and industry team developed a detailed method for the overall process of risk identification, analysis and response used by British Petroleum on many of the company's major studies [24]. The team commented that it requires engineers with appropriate experience and suitable risk analysis training, together with computer software and specialist advice. A single fairly simple study may take two analysts six weeks, plus other staff time for input and review, depending on the objectives of the analysis. Much less work may be adequate if only a few risks are known to be significant, and the analysis much quicker if staff are familiar with using the techniques. A large complex project of long duration may require several updated studies at different points through its life [25].

3.3 Sensitivity analysis

Sensitivity analysis is a technique used to consider the effect on the whole project of changes in the value of each variable which is considered to be a potentially serious risk to the project.

The analysis involves repetitive calculation of the effects on the project outcome of a range of values of the variables. Project outcome is usually considered in terms of speed of construction, final costs or an economic criterion such as Net Present Value (NPV) or Internal Rate of Return (IRR) [26-28]. As an example, assume that one of the risks in a project is the cost of energy and there is a risk that this cost could increase by 5, 10, 15 or 20%. In this analysis the project outcome is recalculated for each of these changes in the cost of energy, and the results can then be represented graphically by plotting the percentage change in the variable against the percentage change in the economic parameter.

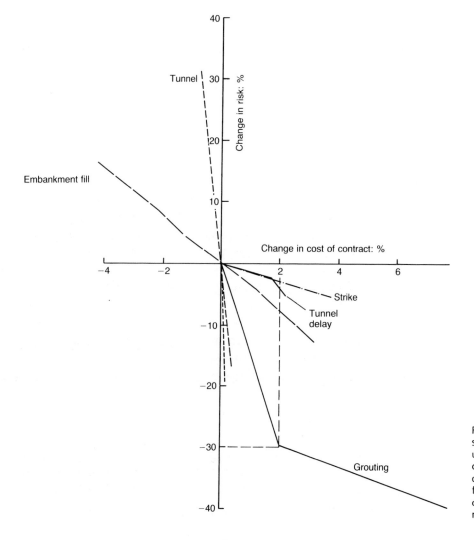

Fig. 5. Dearden Clough Reservoir: sensitivity analysis covering uncertainties in estimated construction cost. A 30% decrease in output when grouting the foundations adds 2% to the total cost of the contract; any greater reduction is far more serious

The results of a sensitivity analysis can be shown graphically on a 'spider diagram' as illustrated in Fig. 5. This example is based upon analysing the possible costs to the contractor of a contract to construct a reservoir. The spider diagram shows the results of calculating the sensitivity of the cost to changes in each risk which could affect productivity on site. For instance, it indicates that a decrease in output when grouting can have a significant effect on the overall cost to the contractor.

The technique is very useful because often the effect of a small change in one variable (a cost or a duration for example) produces a marked difference in the project outcome. When several risks are being assessed in this way, a 'spider diagram' provides a dramatic way of showing the most sensitive or critical risks towards which management must direct its attention [29].

Use of this technique to study the effect of delay in the commissioning of a new industrial plant is described in appendix A of this report.

A sensitivity analysis should be performed for all the risks and uncertainties which may affect a project in order to identify those which have a large impact on the economic return, cost, time, or whatever are the objectives. It can be used to identify the variables which need to be considered for carrying out a probability analysis [30].

A limitation of sensitivity analysis is that each risk is considered independently with no attempt made to quantify their probabilities of occurrence. This technique is also limited because in reality a variable would not change without other project factors changing and this is not reflected in the analysis. With experience, the number of risks to consider can be reduced since those having a large impact on a certain type of project tend to become easily recognisable.

3.4 Probability analysis

Probability analysis overcomes many of the limitations of sensitivity analysis by specifying a *probability distribution* for each risk, and then considering the effects on the risks in combination [31]. The result of the analysis is a range of values in which the final outcome could lie. An essential step in this type of risk analysis is estimating the range of probabilities within which the possible outcomes of a given process may occur [6].

Random ('Monte Carlo') sampling is used where calculation of data inserted into an equation would be difficult or impossible. It is used in a probability analysis in the following way.

- The range of values for the risks being considered are estimated and a suitable probability distribution of each risk is chosen.
- A value for each risk within its specified range is selected; this value should be randomly chosen within the estimated probability distribution.
- The outcome of the project is calculated combining the values selected for each risk.
- The calculation is repeated a number of times to obtain the probability distribution of the project outcome; the number of cycles depends on the degree of confidence required, but 1000 is usually sufficient to make the sampling bias insignificant.

19

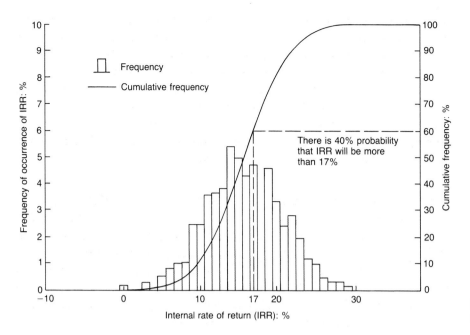

Fig. 6. Mining venture frequency diagram.

The range and probability of the final outcome of the project can be represented graphically, as in Fig.6, where it has been calculated for the internal rate of return from a project. When the main objective of the project is to achieve a specified completion date, a *probabilistic time analysis* can be performed [32]. As the example in Fig. 7 shows, delays in starting a project can reduce the chances of meeting the planned date to practically zero.

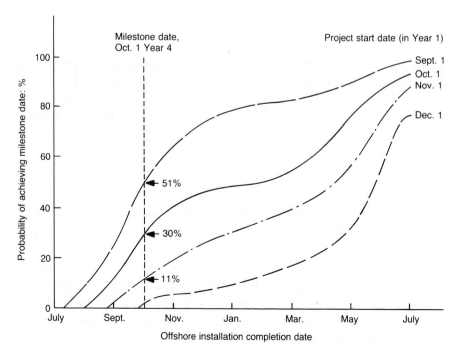

Fig. 7. Probabilistic time analysis applied to the tow-out of the platform for a North Sea oilfield project [33]. If the project were to begin on 1 October in Year 1, the earliest completion date would be August in Year 4, and the probability of completion by the October milestone (the target date) would be 30%

3.5 Simulation of risk

Many programs are now available for analysing and simulating risk, for use on micro-computers. The Association of Project Managers' Specific Interest Group has produced a list of these. We have used and refined our network-based program CASPAR (Computer Aided Simulation for Project Appraisal and Review) to simulate project and contract risk in this research and for the analysis of many real projects [34-36]. It was designed for use in the appraisal stage of projects when there is little objective data available. It can evaluate the consequences of financial and construction risks associated with the engineering, operation and management of the project [37].

Appendix A in this report illustrates the application of CASPAR to a project. This program has been used in the appraisal of many major projects including tidal power schemes in the UK [38-41] and a variety of high-risk projects such as dams and pipelines overseas. It was used to compare alternative methods for the eventual demolition of large North Sea structures [42] and on a risk analysis of part of the cost of the Channel Tunnel, on behalf of EuroTunnel in collaboration with W S Atkins and Setec. Most recently CASPAR has been used in the modelling of BOT projects in Great Britain [43].

The major benefit of these analyses has been in demonstrating robustness to risk and identifying critical uncertainties for further work. The use of this technique in the appraisal of barrage projects showed that one variable considered was of particular importance to the project objectives, in these cases the amount of energy output that would be produced by the facilities in operation. The impact of this risk on the economic viability of the projects was likely to deter funders until the uncertainty was reduced or removed. Further computational and physical modelling therefore followed to improve the accuracy of the data used and so reduce this uncertainty. Action on this was outside the direct control of project management. In the case of other risks, such as contract strategy and actions to avoid delay in construction, management clearly has some control. The studies showed that special attention should be given to the question of who should best act as the client for the construction and operation of a large or unusual project - in other words, who could best minimise and control the delay risk [10,24].

By identifying risks at an early stage, and assessing their relative importance, the management of the projects can be adapted to reduce the risks and allocate them to the parties best able to control them or absorb them should they occur. Studies should be carried out early in the lives of projects well before decisions are made to proceed with them.

3.6 Decision trees

In most major projects there are choices in how to achieve the objectives, so that at the start of the project the decision maker is faced with a variety of alternatives. These alternatives can be shown graphically in a 'decision tree' showing the sequence of known choices and their possible outcomes [27,44,45]. Decision trees are commonly used to study alternative projects and the effects of design and other choices on project costs. Drawing the tree can make the solution obvious. The addition of estimated costs, values of outcomes and probabilities provides a basis for analysing complex problems.

21

This technique can clarify and help communicate a sequence of choices and decisions. It has been used in deciding methods of construction and in contractual problems such as whether to proceed with a claim and assessing the likelihood of a claim succeeding [46]. The technique could be more widely used by clients in choosing between alternative projects and by contractors in choosing between alternative methods of construction.

Decision trees have formed the basis of a number of developments in risk analysis techniques. Project risk models have been developed which combine this with other analytical methods such as probability analysis [25,47] and influence diagrams. A limitation of this technique is that there is rarely sufficient data to calculate accurate probability values for the decision points. Hence it may be advisable to draw a number of decision trees using slightly different probability values. This technique is also limited because the sequence of decision alternatives and the nature of the project are assumed to be static.

22

3.7 Utility theory

The techniques described all attempt to quantify the effects of risk on the project outcome. Once the risks have been analysed it is necessary to interpret the results and to produce a consistent strategy towards risk-taking. At this stage it is necessary to take into account the attitude of the decision makers towards taking risks. A simple example might be the choice between playing safe with a project which guarantees 0.1m, or gambling with a project which has a 20% chance of losing 0.2m and an 80% chance of gaining 1.0m. The problem is that in real decisions the preferences of individuals and corporate decision makers vary greatly.

The concept of utility could be applied to this central problem of decision making under uncertainty - the attitude of decision makers to risk, but in the construction industry utility theory tends to be regarded as a theoretical technique, not easily applied. Hertz & Thomas [30] describe efforts to turn theoretical utility theory into a practical tool. They conclude that, for the present, it is important simply to alert managers to the possibility of bias in decision making.

References

24. C. B. Chapman *et al. Selecting an approach to project time and cost planning. Int. J. Project Manage.*, 1985, **3**, Feb., 19-26.

25. D. F. Cooper and C. B. Chapman. *Risk analysis for large projects*. Wiley, Chichester, 1987.

26. F. H. Knight. *Risk, uncertainty and profit*. Houghton Mifflin, Boston, 1981.

27. A. J. Merrett and A. Sykes. *The finance and analysis of capital projects*. Longman, London, 1983, 2nd edn.

28. P. A. Thompson. *The organization and economics of construction*. McGraw-Hill, London, 1993, 2nd edn.

29. C. Norris. The role of risk analysis in contractual risk allocation. *International Council for Building Research Studies and Documentation (CIB) (W92 - Procurement systems) conference*. Gran Canaria, 1991.

30. D. B. Hertz and H. Thomas. *Risk analysis and its applications*. Wiley, Chichester, 1983.

31. C. B. Chapman. A risk engineering approach to project risk management. *Int. J. Project Manage.*, 1990, **8**, Feb., 5-16.

32. J. N. Hall. The use of risk analysis in North Sea projects. *Int. J. Project Manage.*, 1986, **4**, Nov., 217-222.

33. D. E. Gregg et al. Murchison project preliminary planning organization. *European offshore petroleum conference*. London, 1978.

34. G. Willmer. *Development of risks models for engineering construction projects*. PhD thesis, UMIST, 1988.

35. P. A. Thompson and G. Willmer. CASPAR - a program for engineering project appraisal and management. *Proc. 2nd int. conf. on civil and structural engineering computing*. ICE, London, 1985, vol. 1.

36. G. Willmer. Time and cost risk analysis. *Proc. 4th int. conf. on civil and structural engineering computing*. ICE, London, 1989, vol. 1.

37. C. Norris. *Management of risk in engineering projects*. MSc thesis, UMIST, 1992.

38. UMIST. *Severn tidal power: sensitivity and risk analysis*. Project Management Group, UMIST, 1980.

39. J. G. Perry *et al*. *Mersey barrage pre-feasibility study*. Marinetech North West, University of Manchester, 1983, vols 1-3.

40. *Mersey barrage - a re-examination of the economics*. Marinetech North West and Rendel-Parkman for Merseyside County Council.

41. G. Willmer. Time and cost risk analysis. *Comput. Struct.*, 1991, **41**, No. 6, 1149-1155.

42. S. H. Wearne *et al*. *North Sea platform decommissioning and removal: technical developments priorities study*. Marinetech North West and UMIST Project Management Group, 1987.

43. A. Merna and N. J. Smith. The allocation of risks in BOT contracts. *International Council for Building Research Studies and Documentation (CIB) (W92 - Procurement systems) conferences*. Gran Canaria, 1991.

44. M. W. Lifson and E. F. Shaifer. *Decision and risk analysis for construction management*. Wiley, Chichester, 1982.

45. P. D. Newendorp. *Decision analysis for petroleum exploration*. Petroleum Publishing Co., Tulsa, 1975.

46. D. B. Ashley *et al*. Critical decision making during construction. *J. Construct. Engng Manage.*, 1983, **109**, June, 146-162.

47. C. B. Chapman and D. F. Cooper. Risk analysis: testing some prejudices. *Eur. J. Oper. Res.*, 1983, **14**, 238-247.

Risk in estimating

4

The reason for producing any estimate of cost and time for a project is to predict the final total cost and completion date as accurately as possible so that the client knows what to expect. To achieve this, all risks which might affect the cost or progress of work must be identified and allowed for in the estimate. Some may be eliminated or reduced and some are outside the control of the project management, but all of them should be considered. Ignoring or excluding a real risk, because for instance it is outside the control of management, can deceive everyone involved.

Clients usually require a first estimate early in proposals for a project, when there may be many uncertainties and some may be very large in their possible effects. The requirement to estimate cost despite having only limited data early highlights a problem common to all estimating - how should uncertainty be allowed for ?

4.1 Refining the original estimate

Research has shown that many client organisations, including some with a sophisticated policy on project risk management or who employ risk management consultants, keep the estimating function separate from the risk management function. This situation prohibits estimating realism and limits the success of the risk management process.

Perhaps because of a lack of systematic attention to risk when estimating, the most common method of allowing for uncertainty is to add a percentage figure to the 'most likely' estimate of final cost [48]. The amount added is usually called *contingency*. To provide the base for this addition the 'most likely' estimate should therefore exclude any risk contingency (the estimate of most likely cost is also known as a 'best' estimate).

This widely used method has several weaknesses.

- The percentage figure is, most likely, arbitrarily arrived at and not appropriate for the specific project.
- There is a tendency to double-count risk because some estimators are inclined to include contingencies in their 'best' estimate.

4.2 Estimating and risk analysis

- A percentage addition still results in a single-figure prediction of estimated cost, implying a degree of certainty that is simply not justified.
- The percentage added indicates the potential for detrimental or 'downside' risk; it does not indicate any potential for cost reduction, and may therefore hide poor management of the execution of the project.
- Because the percentage allows for all risk in terms of a cost contingency, it tends to direct attention away from time, performance and quality risks.
- It does not encourage creativity in estimating practice, allowing it to become routine and mundane, which can propagate oversights.

Instead, some clients take the original estimate and apply a variety of methods of allowing contingencies for risk. These include

- using estimating manuals containing risk checklists with contingency ranges defined for each risk
- refining the estimate by reference to historical project cost data bases and correlation with current input prices
- identifying specific risks and allocating contingencies to those risks; the contingency amounts can be released only by pre-defined events specified in the risk management strategy
- building and using a project risk model using risk analysis software, as indicated in chapter 3.

Whichever method of applying contingencies is adopted, a major factor in its success in predicting future cost, duration and quality is that it must be governed by a well-structured risk analysis and risk management strategy. Those members of the client organisation responsible for considering risk should therefore be involved in the estimating for a project from its very beginning [49].

4.3 Risk allowances

Risk allowances comprise contingencies and tolerances. The use of these two words varies in practice, but we distinguish between them as follows.

- **Contingencies** - allowances added to an estimate to represent the best judgement of undefined or uncertain items of work which it is considered should be provided for.
- **Tolerances** - the range of values above and below the estimated project cost, duration or performance within which the final value is likely to fall.

Contingencies are 'areas of space' in an estimate which help a project manager to meet the project cost, time and performance objectives, as they face exposure to project risk and uncertainty [50]. Separate contingency allowances should be provided for each specific item of work which is undefined or uncertain, to provide the basis for budgeting and control.

Tolerances are derived from two sources: firstly the accuracy of estimating the costs and durations of activities; secondly the uncertainty due to the identified risks. The result is estimates in terms of ranges of values, not single values.

4.4 Risk exposure

The client may not wish the ranges to be wide enough allow for every possible worst (or best) outcome that may occur. For instance, he may wish to set limits for estimating purposes on the extent of exchange rate fluctuations or may not wish the time and cost effects of severe flooding or earthquake to be allowed for in the estimate. Or a contractor under the commercial pressures of tendering may deliberately decide not to allow contingencies or tolerances for some risks in his bid.

This leads to a further concept.

- **Risk exposure** - the amount of risk still not allowed for financially.

Any estimate should state the items excluded from it, and ideally should indicate the resulting risk exposure.

Ideally the amounts of contingency and tolerance that are set at the identification and appraisal stages of a project should be high enough to give a reasonable upper limit for the project. Then as risks and uncertainties are removed or reduced the contingency and tolerances should reduce [51,52]. Fig. 8 shows the so-called torpedo or projectile effect of risks on cost predictions.

This diagram illustrates the value of range estimating. This is one of the concepts which we recommend to politicians and their advisers for inclusion in the procedures for sanctioning and controlling public works projects.

4.5 Reduction stage-by-stage through a project

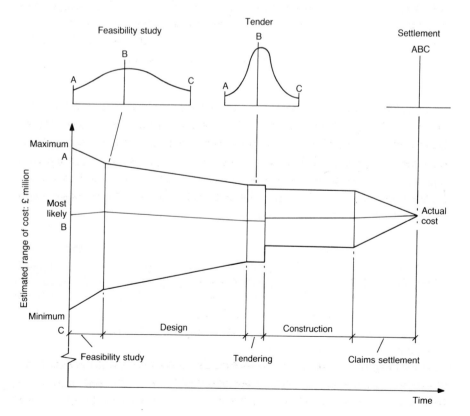

Fig. 8. Probability distributions of cost estimates stage-by-stage through a project. Probabilities and uncertainties in cost prediction vary from stage-to-stage. The diagram illustrates continually lessening uncertainty in predicting final cost

4.6 Purposes of estimates

Risk analysis and risk management consultants devote a lot of resources to educating clients about the relationship between risk and estimates, and the effects of client decisions on them. It is important to be clear about the different purposes of estimates for a project and how they should be evolved.

The types of cost estimate needed by clients will differ according to individual organisation requirements. We consider that the following are essential for predicting and controlling the cost of projects.

4.7 Feasibility estimate

Typically relatively little data is available for the feasibility studies of a project. Decisions at this stage are therefore exposed to maximum levels of uncertainty. Without expenditure to obtain data, risk cannot be considered in a systematic way.

An estimate compiled with such limited data is generally called a 'ball-park' figure. Deriving it is best based on a combination of experienced engineering and estimating judgement, drawing on previous project data where available.

The result should be presented as a range of figures, with prominence being placed upon the upper limit. In some organizations there is a danger that a single figure receives undue respect and becomes fixed in the minds of senior management, dominating all subsequent expectations. To avoid this the sensitivity of the figures to the input data [53] and the level of confidence in the accuracy of the figures should be stated.

27

4.8 Budget estimate

Once a project has been shown to satisfy the client's feasibility criteria, it may then be considered for inclusion in the capital budget plan. The business must formulate a capital investment programme, which requires a forward view of capital demand. At this stage clients are generally willing to spend more to define the scope of possible projects and to pay for preliminary design work in order to obtain the basis for more accurate estimates.

Again it should be emphasised that the feasibility estimate may dominate this definition of scope. This estimate may have been presented as a single figure for budgeting purposes. Preferably it should be prepared on a range basis to indicate uncertainty. The capital figure which may then be used for a budget is then a management decision, dependent upon market factors and corporate philosophy. However the range estimate provides decision makers with a more realistic view of potential project costs.

4.9 Sanction estimate

This estimate provides the basis for the commitment of resources to the project. At this phase the scope of the project should have been defined and a significant part of the design completed. Risk can then be considered in a systematic way, with a well-defined risk analysis and risk management strategy.

The accuracy of the sanction estimate should be expressed in terms of a tolerance upon the 'best' estimate and the contingencies allowed. The contingencies and their purpose should be clearly expressed. The tolerance should depend upon the perceived uncertainty remaining at the time and should not be an arbitrary percentage figure.

4.10 Audit estimate

When the project is completed there should be an analysis of its actual cost, time and performance. This should detail all expenditure and the reason for each item. It should list all those identified risks that did occur and show their effects, and the same for those which occurred but were not previously identified. Since it is impracticable to try to be completely accurate, the results of the review should still be regarded as estimates.

The data obtained is very valuable for the development and control of subsequent projects and should be added to other historical data to aid estimating judgements. It can provide a basis for assessing project management performance. It is also valuable for training estimators.

4.11 Managing cost, time and quality

Despite a growing realisation in project management of the dependent relationship between the cost, time and quality objectives, invariably only cost contingencies are considered as a viable means of allowing for risk. It is possible to include space for all three.

Cost - cost contingencies and tolerances

Time - float and tolerances in the programme

Performance - 'space' in the specification

To a limited extent these may be traded by the project manager as the project evolves. For example, acceleration in programmes can be bought, and cost saved or delay avoided by accepting work which does not meet specification on non-essential items. The extent to which these can be traded may change during a project, and so may the relative importance of cost, time and quality.

Manipulation of contingencies of cost and time can be useful to promote motivation. It demands risk awareness in project managers.

Good management may be needed to overcome a common perception that 'if contingencies are set they will be used' ! [54] If this is the case, as it is in some organizations, the fault lies not in the setting of the contingencies but in the control and allocation of the project resources. The squandering of project funds is a symptom of poor project management rather than poor estimating. It is important to realise that the contingencies required in project estimates are closely linked to the efficiency with which the project resources are allocated and managed.

Techniques of the type described have been developed with the aims of reducing underestimates, providing greater appreciation of the impact of potential risks, and establishing methods of quantifying the effects of risks. During the research we have encountered arguments that the data or time needed to prepare a realistic estimate are not available in the early stages of the project, and that despite the best efforts of project managers this situation will recur in the future.

If so, the project managers have to ensure that the limitations of such estimates are emphasised throughout the organisation. Increases in cost when the project is more clearly defined are the usual result, and a project may need to be re-appraised to review its viability.

Arbitrary reductions of an estimate or of tolerances have the same result. They inevitably lead to increased costs later.

References

48. J. R. Healy. Contingency funds evaluation. *Trans. Am. Assoc. Cost Engnrs*, 1982, B3.1-B3.4.

49. UMIST. *A guide to cost estimating for overseas construction projects*. Project Management Group, UMIST, for the Overseas Development Administration, 1989.

50. L. Mulekezi. *Research in progress on contingencies and risk estimating*. University of Birmingham, School of Civil Engineering.

51. N. M. L. Barnes (S. H. Wearne (Ed.)). *Control of engineering projects*. Thomas Telford, London, 1989, chap. 4.

52. J. Morris (N. M. L. Barnes (Ed.)). *Financial control*. Thomas Telford, London, 1990, chap. 4.

53. K. T. Yeo. Project cost sensitivity and variability analysis. *Int. J. Project Manage.*, 1991, **9**, May, 111-116.

54. W. R. Querns. What is contingency anyway? *Trans. Am. Assoc. Cost Engnrs*, 1989, B9.1-B9.5.

Contract strategy

5

Early in the development of a project the client has to make decisions on technical choices such as size, location and standards. He should also then make decisions on a contract strategy, that is how best to employ contractors for construction and other services.

To decide a strategy the client needs to have defined

- his objectives - the priorities between project cost, construction time, quality and any secondary objectives.
- the roles and authority of his project manager, the project designers and the client's own direct labour resources (if any).

5.1 Basis of a strategy

Selecting the contract strategy requires decisions about

- number of work packages and whether there should be one main contractor or several contractors [55];
- division of tasks between the client's project team, consultants and contractors, particularly who is to be responsible for design, materials, construction and services;
- terms of payment;
- basis for selecting contractors.

In the past there were few options for contract strategy, now there are many. The choice between them should aim to give the maximum likelihood of achieving the client's objectives.

5.2 Decisions

Choices on the above should be made by considering the implications for managing the project.

- How much control does the client wish to exert?
- What flexibility is needed for changes during construction?
- What will motivate contractors?
- How should risk be best allocated?

5.3 Implications for project management

- Special site conditions.
- Control of sub-contracting and purchasing.
- Cash flow of client and contractors.
- Responsibilities for action on defective work.
- Procedure for dealing with variations.
- Reports and other information required by client.
- Time needed to prepare tender documents and select between tenderers.

Consideration of all the above should lead to the choice of the appropriate set of conditions of contract for a project. These general terms of a contract are the primary vehicle for defining the allocation of risk between all parties.

5.4 Attention to risk

Lack of a contract strategy based upon attention to risk can produce very unpleasant surprises that lead to later protracted disputes. For example, when contractors are faced with managing major contract risks their tender prices and the final contract durations and prices are often disturbingly out of line with the client's initial expectations. The parties to a contract are also frequently at odds over the interpretation of risk allocation in the contract and the responsibility for managing the risks (or carrying the consequences of the risk). The result has been the rapid growth of the 'claims industry', contract arbitration and litigation, in building and in civil engineering in the UK, USA, and some Commonwealth countries.

From such experience many project managers and observers have concluded that traditional contract strategies for construction and their allocation of responsibilities and risks in standard conditions of contract are inappropriate for today's higher risk and complex projects. A tailor-made contract strategy suitable for the active management of risk by all parties is seen as more suitable. A study in the USA has shown that 5% of project cost may be saved by choice of the most appropriate terms of contract alone [56]. Research with the industry and a NEDO committee have emphasised the benefits of unconventional contracts for high risk projects [57-59]. Perry [60] has developed a systematic method for the preparation of a contract strategy taking into account the influence of risk. The opportunity to manage risk through contract strategy decisions should not be undervalued.

References

55. S. H. Wearne. *Civil engineering contracts*. Thomas Telford, London, 1989.

56. The Business Round Table. *Contractual arrangements: a construction industry cost effectiveness report*. USA, 1982.

57. J. G. Perry *et al*. *Target and cost-reimbursable construction contracts*. CIRIA, London, 1982, report 85.

58. NEDO. *Target cost contracts - a worthwhile alternative*. The National Economic Development Office, London, 1982.

59. R. W. Hayes *et al*. *Management contracting*. CIRIA, London, 1983, report 100.

60. J. G. Perry. *The development of contract strategies for construction projects*. PhD thesis, UMIST, 1985.

31

Dealing with risk in contracts

6

6.1 Formulating the contract

Careful analysis for a contract strategy should lead to the selection of the right allocation of responsibilities, type of contract and tendering procedure for a project. To proceed with preparing the contract requires the identification of specific risks, decisions on how the risks are to be shared between the parties, and the definition of the risk allocation in the draft contract documents.

The most challenging of these tasks is deciding what is the equitable risk allocation. The availability of 'model' (or 'standard') sets of general conditions of contract has held back clear thinking about risk allocation. Risk is allocated in these models, but the principles behind the allocations have not been stated. The various models also differ in allocating risk, and problems can arise using any of them if additional clauses affecting risk are applied to them.

6.2 Traditional contracts for construction

Traditionally the risk in construction projects is allocated as follows

- client to designer and contractor
- contractor to subcontractors
- client, designer, contractor and subcontractors to insurers
- contractor and subcontractors to sureties or guarantors.

6.3 Principles for risk allocation

Following the work by Ashley [61,8], Porter [62], Barnes [63], Abrahamson [64], and Perry and Hayes [65], we recommend these principles for the allocation of risk among the parties to a project.

- Which party can best control the events that may lead to the risk occurring?
- Which party can best manage the risk if it occurs?
- Whether or not it is preferable for the client to retain an involvement in the management of the risk.
- Which party should carry the risk if it cannot be controlled?
- Whether the premium to be charged by the transferee is likely to be reasonable and acceptable.
- Whether the transferee is likely to be able to sustain the consequences if the risk occurs.

- Whether, if the risk is transferred, it leads to the possibility of risks of a different nature being transferred back to the client.

Applying these principles may lead managers away from many model conditions of contract. If traditional models are used it is important to appreciate their limitations. For example, in the Institution of Civil Engineers Conditions of Contract [66] payment to the contractor can be different to the tender price for three reasons

- remeasurement of actual quantities of work completed and payment for them at the tendered rates
- changes in the nature or content of the work ordered by the engineer
- claims submitted by the contractor for extension of time and/or additional payment arising from delay, disruption or unexpected conditions.

These terms in the ICE contract will allow for perhaps a 20% variation in contract price. Some improvement can be achieved by paying separate method-related charges for disruption or delay and 'contract price fluctuations' for cost inflation, but even with these provisions the ICE terms often lead to disputes, and where there is greater uncertainty they tend to become unworkable.

33

6.4 Terms of payment

Risks are allocated differently in contracts which are 'cost-based' than in those which are 'price-based'. The way in which risk is *paid for* distinguishes these two main types of contract [60].

Price-based contracts include fixed price (usually lump sum paid) and unit price contracts (using a bill of quantities or a schedule of rates). Payment is based on the prices or rates submitted by the contractor in his tender. These are usually deemed to include all the contractor's costs, overheads, risk contingencies and profit. These contracts thus require the contractor to carry a greater proportion of risks than cost-based contracts, as shown in Table 2. Before tendering the contractor should estimate the costs of the risks he is to carry and include them in his price or rates, in the form of a hidden risk contingency, as only for the reasons listed above in section 6.3 will the contractor will be entitled to some additional payment.

The uncertainties of risk and claims, coupled with the confidentiality of the contractor's costs, make the adequacy of the payment little more than a gamble to parties. When the extent of risk and uncertainty is high this may become a major gamble, with clients possibly paying excessive amounts for their contracts. The more likely outcome is that contractors will be seriously underpaid - even to the extent of forcing them out of business before completing a contract.

The alternative of cost-based contracts includes cost-reimbursable plus fee and target-cost variants [57,58]. In these, the majority of or all risks are paid for by the client. He will pay the actual costs required to deal with risk or uncertainty and these will be known to him through the open-book accounts. As a result, the contractor should always be fairly reimbursed. Unless appropriate controls are introduced, the client may feel he is paying excessive amounts, due to the alleged lack of incentive for the contractor to perform efficiently. Consequently, the client will usually require greater involvement in the control of the contractor's costs.

Table 2. Risk implications of different terms of payment to contractors

	FIXED PRICE	UNIT PRICE	TARGET COST	COST REIMBURSED
Financial objectives of client and contractor	Different but reasonably independent	Different and in potential conflict	Considerable harmony, reduction of actual cost is a common objective if cost remains in the incentive range	Both based on actual cost but potentially in conflict
Flexibility for design changes and variations	Very limited	Some	Extensive	Unlimited
Evaluation of change by client	Little or no information in tender	Mainly based on tendered rates	Target adjustment for based on actual costs and use of resources or target rates	Unnecessary contractual purposes
Overlap of design and construction, early start to construction	Not practicable	Feasible but relatively limited	Considerable opportunity	Construction may be started when first design package is available
Contractor involved in design of permanent works	Excluded	Usually excluded	Contractor encouraged to contributefor ideas for cost saving	Contractor can be appointed design input prior to construction
Client influence on construction management	Excluded	Retrospective	Recommended through joint planning	Should be active
Payment for risk	Undisclosed contingency in tender	Undisclosed contingency in tender plus claims	Payment of actual cost if risk occurs	Payment of actual cost
Claims resolution	No basis for evaluation	Client has no knowledge of actual cost or contingency	Based on actual cost or target cost, mechanism needs careful drafting	Unnecessary except for adjustment of fee
Knowledge of final price at tender (excluding inflation)	Known	Uncertain - tender price usually increased by variations and claims	Uncertain - tender target usually changed by variations and savings	Unknown

One means of control is the use of a target-cost contract to provide an incentive to the contractor to keep actual costs low in order to beat the target and gain a share of the difference. The research commissioned by the Construction Industry Research & Information Association reported on 25 cases of this type of contract [57]. More recent studies in North America and in the UK have reported on the success of the consequent development of *partnering* rather than adversarial relationships between client and contractor [67,68]. In Australia there has been a similar development towards dispute-free contracts [69]. How attention to risk should influence the choice of type of contract in the example of a major road project in Third World countries is shown in Table 3 [70].

6.5 Contract management

The client and his advisers must choose how the *responsibilities* for design, construction and supporting activities are to be allocated and integrated. The traditional approach in the UK centres on the role of 'the Engineer' or 'the Architect' named in the contract and the contractual liabilities of the main contractor, with well-known strengths and limitations in controlling a project [71].

Today there are many alternative organisational structures from which to choose. Fee contracting, management contracts, construction management, design-and-management, and design-and-build are all used, and each allocates risk in a different way. This is achieved partly through the method of payment as described above. In addition, there may be special conditions of contract, particularly in management contracts.

A newer development are build-operate-transfer (BOT) and build-own-operate-transfer contracts (BOOT) in which the client grants a concession to a contractor or a joint venture project company for the

- financing
- design
- construction

operation and maintenance of a facility [72-77].

Examples of large BOT projects include the Channel Tunnel and the Dartford Crossing. At the end of a pre-determined period, the asset is transferred to the client free of charge and in good operating condition. During the operation phase, the contractor or joint venture project company recoups its capital investment and operating costs and, it hopes, makes a profit from revenues generated by the operation of the asset (for instance, tolls at the Dartford Crossing). Many clients have seen the BOT model as a means of transferring more risk to the private sector. Clearly the participants in a BOT project will need to pay close attention to risk management strategies.

Probably the greatest implications for risk management in these non-traditional contractual arrangements comes from the management structure and in particular the responsibilities given to management. In most of the arrangements cited above, the contractor is involved in the pre-construction phase, and the management of design and construction is integrated.

How effective are these methods in producing an overall risk reduction to the client? There is a need for more hard evidence, but some indication was gained recently in the *Faster Building for Industry* report [3] - 'on average non-traditional techniques of management tend to be quicker'. In other words, they produced a reduction in the risk of time overrun, and the report concluded that this did not necessarily lead to additional costs. Our study of management and target cost contracts tends to support this important finding.

6.6 Conditions of contract

The *Faster Building* report concluded that 'it is not the form of contract which primarily determines whether targets are met, but the attitudes of the parties to which the form of contract may contribute - industry and customer should look

ENGINEERING CONSTRUCTION RISKS

Table 3. *Risks and problems with a Third World road project [70]*

Logistical

Transport of labour and staff to site
The need for a transport convoy
Heavy dependence on aircraft for transport of key people and communication
Telephone link some three hours drive from site
Shortage of trained operators and skilled labour in a rural area
Severe security problems
Unpredictable amount of rainfall and extent of wet season
Loss of efficiency of plant at altitude
Need to provide own utilities such as power, drainage, and water treatment

Technical

Based on preliminary designs and unproven sources of materials
Instability of pink soils
Increased extent of cut/fill
Need for 75km of diversion road
Extra drainage and scour protection
Longer hauls for gravels than anticipated
Original plant inappropriate because of greatly increased use of lime-stabilised base

for ways of sharing the benefit from improved performance'.

There are two lessons here. Firstly, existing models do not greatly help the achievements of objectives, i.e. they do not make a significant contribution to reducing the effects of risk. Secondly, new or improved contract models should be developed which contain incentives for performance and are designed for risk management. It can be argued that the existing models have stood the test of time. It may also be said that they have become outdated, too rigid and too detailed. Model conditions of contract can make a valuable contribution to risk management if they have the following characteristics

- clear definitions of risk and their allocations
- improved incentives linked to risk allocation
- flexibility for different allocations of risk
- designed for effective contract management of time, cost, safety and quality.

While this report was being prepared the draft *New Engineering Contract* model set of conditions of contract was issued by the Institution of Civil Engineers, initially for comment [78,79]. This contains several advances on earlier models in relation to the analysis and allocation of risk.

6.7 New Engineering Contract

- It requires the user to choose his preferred contract strategy. This should achieve attention to the differences in the allocation of risk between various strategies.
- It contains, in one list, a standard risk allocation between client and contractor and also permits a tailored allocation of special risks.
- It defines a single procedure for compensating the contractor when a risk occurs.
- It is designed to be simpler to read and understand than most other models.

One of the aims of the NEC is to reduce the extent of disputes, on and off site, which arise from unclear or uncertain procedures in contracts. It has been designed on the basis of many of the principles set out in this report. By stating clearly the risks and the responsibilities for managing them it is intended that the overall management of risk will be seen to be much more the task of engineers and project managers and less that of lawyers and insurers.

Any means of reducing disputes and the amounts of money under dispute in the construction industry is worthy of attention.

References

61. D. B. Ashley. *Construction project risk sharing*. Stanford University, Construction Institute, 1977, technical report 220.

62. C. E. Porter. *Risk allocation in construction contracts*. MSc thesis, UMIST, 1981.

63. N. M. L. Barnes. How to allocate risks in construction contracts. *Int. J. Project Manage.*, 1983, **1**, Feb., 24-28.

64. M. W. Abrahamson. Risk management. *Int. Construct. Law. Rev.*, 1984, **1**, Apr., 241-264.

65. J. G. Perry and R. W. Hayes. Risk and its management in construction projects. *Proc. Instn Civ. Engrs*, Part 1, 1985, **78**, 499-521.

66. ICE. *Conditions of contract and forms of tender, agreement and bond for use in connection with works of civil engineering construction*. ICE, London, 1991, 6th edn.

67. Construction Industry Institute. *In search of partnering excellence*. CII, Texas, 1991, special publication 17-1.

68. NEDO. *Partnering: contracting without conflict*. The National Economic Development Office, 1991.

69. No dispute: strategies for improvement in the Australian building and construction industry. *National Public Works conference*, Australia, 1990.

70. P. A. Thompson and J. G. Perry. *The operation of the target-cost contract for the construction of the Makambako - Wino road, Tanzania*. Overseas Development Administration, London, 1984, evaluation report EV249.

71. G. E. Ninos and S. H. Wearne. Control of projects during construction. *Proc. Instn Civ. Engnrs*, Part 1, 1986, **80**, Aug., 931-943; 1987, **82**, 859-869.

72. S. C. McCarthy and J. G. Perry. BOT contracts for water supply. *World water '89 conference*. Thomas Telford, London, 1990, 125-130.

73. S. C. McCarthy. BOT for tomorrow's infrastructure. *Independent Consulting Engineer*, 1991.

74. S. C. McCarthy and R. L. K. Tiong. Financial and contractual aspects of build-operate-transfer projects. *Int. J. Project Manage.*, 1991, **4**, Nov., 222-227.

75. S. C. McCarthy. *BOT and OMT contracts for infrastructure projects in developing countries*. PhD thesis, University of Birmingham, 1991.

76. S. C. McCarthy *et al*. Critical success factors for winning BOT contracts. *J. Construct. Engng Manage.*, to be published.

77. S. C. McCarthy. Management and allocation of risks in BOT projects. *11th INTERNET conference*. Florence, 1992.

78. ICE. *New engineering contract*. Institution of Civil Engineers, London, 1991.

79. N. M. L. Barnes. New engineering contract. *Int. Construct. Law Rev.*, 1991, **8**, Apr., 247-255.

37

Tenders - the risks to clients and contractors

7.1 Competitive tendering

Competitive tendering has had the effect of preventing a realistic attitude towards risk. Even when some provision has been made for eventualities it is often buried in the total bid. Unless the risks are small, clients should endeavour to ensure pre-contract that all bidders have understood the risks allocated to them and have made appropriate provision in their bids. If the risks are large, clients should consider stating the allocation of risk in the tender documents and require bidders to specify the provision for risks in their bids.

Appendix B shows how a contractor can apply quantitative techniques to assess risk when tendering.

When the tender documents for a contract lead contractors into believing that a large or unclear amount of risk is to be taken by them, the result can be fewer bidders, and a wide spread of bid prices. This is partly because each contractor includes a different sum for risk contingencies. This promotes the gambling aspects of price-based bidding. A reduction in the arbitrary nature of pricing should help the entire construction industry.

When tenders are received from contractors, the opportunity for risk reduction or avoidance is limited and the decisions on risk transfer have already been made. In cases where the client has actually opted to retain the risks, allowances must be made in his estimate for all possible risks. In most contracts these include inflation and, on overseas contracts, exchange rate variations.

7.2 Residual risk

The level of risk *retention* by the client associated with tenders should not be under-estimated. For instance, a fixed price contract may be effective in controlling costs, but it may reduce the client's control and can lead to time overruns and knock-on costs. The resultant loss of benefit to the client is unlikely to be fully recoverable by him.

Tender amounts and the final contract value are also at risk. There is always the possibility of physical change due to unforeseen ground conditions, exceptional weather conditions or design changes to cope with changed functional requirements. Bidders may also have a limited time to prepare their tenders. They may not therefore identify all potential risks, or analyse them thoroughly, and contractual loopholes and market conditions tempt them to bid low with a reasonable hope of recovering additional money through claims. And, in competitive tendering, it is most unlikely that the lowest bidder has covered all his potential risks. The more risks there are to consider, the more likelihood of omissions.

In spite of the allocation of risks through the contract, any significant default by the contractor remains the client's risk. The client's budget should therefore be based upon a prediction of the final achieved cost of the project, including allowances for the serious risks which the contractor may not have included in his tender.

7.3 Evaluating tenders

There are many examples of contracts in which the lowest bid did not result in the lowest final price. Selecting a contractor on price alone has amounted to buying trouble. To be able to anticipate this the client should use risk analysis to decide what range of prices is reasonable.

If contractors are bidding for a high risk contract the client should consider setting a 'minimum acceptable risk' contract price below which a bidder will not be awarded the contract, as proposed by Inyang and Willmer [80]. It is not new for bids to be rejected on the basis of price being unrealistically low. A risk analysis can establish a quantitative basis for doing so, if done for each particular high-risk project. A standard rule that the acceptable range is the prices that lie within the mean value ± one standard deviation could become known to bidders and itself influence prices.

Whatever price is chosen, the client should then be clear in his mind what the level of risk is, and he should be satisfied that the contract has not been awarded to a contractor taking an unreasonable risk.

Reference

80. E. D. Inyang and G. Willmer. Practical considerations in the solution of probabilistic risk analysis models for engineering project management decision making. *Proc. int. conf. on advances in engineering management (EMTA '86)*. Swansea, 1986.

Risk and overseas projects 8

Competent risk management can be critical to obtaining work overseas. The risks of projects in Third World countries are usually larger than those of corresponding ones in the UK. They need attention before any commitment to any clients, government or prospective partners [21]. The allowance for risk is therefore often the largest single item of cost in a contractor's tender for a project overseas [81].

Overseas clients and the international funding banks tend to be less tolerant of cost overruns, and many are not aware of or may be dubious about the advantages of traditional British contract practice [82,83].

8.1 Overseas differences

International conferences and organizations responsible for international conditions of contract such as FIDIC (the Fédération International des Ingénieurs-Conseils) indicate a decreasing influence of British practice and procedures overseas. The innovative contracting practices in the UK noted in the previous chapter and aggressive marketing of these may help redress this.

For example, management contracting may prove to be a powerful means of meeting the needs of overseas clients, by involving them more closely in construction management and decision-making, and making the most of local firms and labour. Using smaller local firms which are not yet capable of taking the main contractor role but have access to relatively cheap labour can provide a competitive advantage.

As mentioned earlier, the target cost type of contract has had success on overseas projects [57,70] in getting contracts finished on time, and by increasing the number of contractors who are willing to bid because of the reduction in their risks. Design-and-build contracts which allow clients to vary the role of 'the architect' could also be more widely marketed.

The development of such flexible and risk-reducing contract forms in the UK should enable us to take a lead in promoting efficient and effective contract systems which meet the needs of overseas clients.

8.2 Contract practices

References

81. D. E. Cullivan. How much will it cost. *Consult. Engr*, 1981, Feb., 13.

82. ICE. *Management of international construction projects*. Institution of Civil Engineers, London, 1985.

83. ICE. *Overseas projects - critical problems*. Institution of Civil Engineers, London, 1988.

41

The role of project management

Engineering project management has a vital role to play in risk management. In the work leading up to approval of funds, project managers can contribute to economic decisions by producing realistic estimates of cost and time which are based on a clear specification of operational and quality requirements [49].

During the project their role is to ensure that risks to cost, time and performance are managed so as to meet the client's objectives [51].

What should project managers be looking at to achieve these aims ? We believe that success comes by

- thorough study of risk and uncertainty, stage by stage through all but minor projects

- using estimates of cost and time which include specific contingency allowances and show ranges representing the major risks and uncertainties

- proposals to at least reduce the effects of risk and uncertainty

- adoption of methods for allocating the remaining risks to the various parties in a way which will optimise the results for the project

- recognition that risk and reward go hand-in-hand and that the allocation of a risk to a party should be accompanied by a motivation for good management

- open-minded interest in innovative solutions to problems

- special awareness of the problems of overseas clients

- regular and preferably independent review of project proposals and conceptual design to reduce misunderstandings and to try to ensure that all potential uncertainties are exposed.

In this report we have described some of the techniques that are now available to help project managers apply these guidelines.

Appendix A: Project risk case study

The 'New Industrial Plant' project

The hypothetical 'New Industrial Plant' project is used as a case to illustrate how risk may be analysed and how this process can aid the perception of risk.

The client expected that the project would take 3 years from appraisal to the completion of construction, and that the productive life of the resulting facility would be 10 years, making a total life cycle of 13 years. These periods are taken as the 'base' for assessing the likely profitability of the project and the potential effects of delays and other possible risks.

The analysis

The risk analysis is performed as part of the appraisal prior to sanction when only conceptual design has been developed and there are many uncertainties.

The case shows that much can be learned about the implications and management of risk in a project without extensive numerical analysis using computers, by what is essentially a brain-storming process to compile a simple but realistic time and money flowchart of the project, followed by consideration of appropriate 'what happens if' questions.

The model

A time-cost model of the project is used to simulate the implications of alternative patterns of project development and to predict the consequences of risk in terms of the effect on the investment. It is designed to show the interactive relationships between time and cash flow and to give a realistic response in terms of cash flow to changes of all the variables considered.

The details of the model used are described elsewhere [28]. It is based on a precedence network of only 20 activities or work packages and incorporates production forecasts as shown in Fig.9.

The realism of the modelling is greatly dependent on the correct allocation of costs and revenues to each activity. Costs must be prescribed in the way and time at which they are incurred, i.e. as fixed costs, time-related or quantity-proportional.

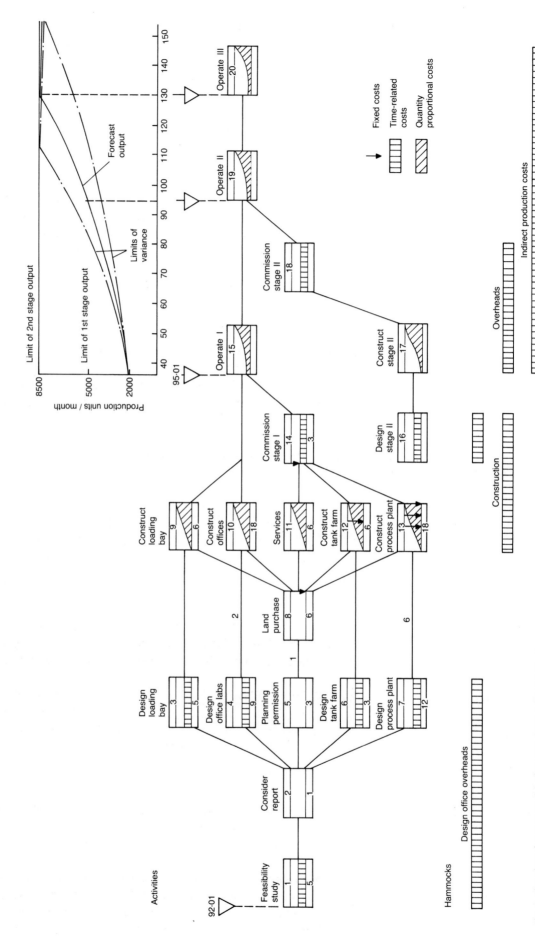

Fig. 9. Flowchart for cost model of New Industrial Plant project

When compiling the flowchart and basic model the most likely predictions and estimates should be used, and all assumptions and exclusions should be stated.

This is a 'paper-and-pencil' exercise. We recommend that it should involve all persons responsible for providing estimates or other predictions. After that the data can be put into a computer program such as CASPAR in order to be able to simulate the effects of changes [36,37].

The 'best' estimate

The base case forecast of cumulative cash flow of the project is shown in Fig.10. The base case excluding interest payments indicates a cash surplus of 88m at the end of the planned project life. The payback period is under 6 years. The IRR (internal rate of return) is 36.8%. The effect of interest payments is that the payback period is increased by 9 months and the IRR reduced to 31.26%.

These returns from the project will of course be achieved only if all the predictions and estimates over the 13 years of appraisal, implementation and operation of the project are precisely fulfilled !

A variety of financial criteria, including both cash and discounted values, can be used to quantify the investment. Non-escalated cost and revenue values have been used above. We recommend that inflation is considered separately throughout risk analysis, as it can introduce additional long term uncertainty [84].

Consideration of risk and uncertainty

It is likely that there will be uncertainty about many of the predictions used in the base model, and these will now be investigated.

At this stage it is possible to obtain an indication of the implication of these uncertainties simply by 'doodling' - substituting different values for variables in the original model, recalculating the cost and benefit, and sketching the new cash flow curve. This repetitive exercise can be used to predict the effect of delay in commissioning or a change in market forecasts even if a full risk analysis using a computer is not attempted.

Particular attention should be paid to risk and expenditure at the end of the operating life of the facility. The cost of decommissioning may be significant in cash terms but can be easily overlooked if only discounted figures are studied !

The risk arising from the market or demand for the service or product may be reduced by staging the development of the project. Implementation of a second stage of 'New Industrial Plant' could depend on the actual production figures achieved following the commissioning of a first stage.

Sensitivity to the estimates

The consequences of changes in the values of selected variables and their relative significance in terms of effect on the IRR of the project are well-illustrated in the sensitivity diagram Fig.11 produced using CASPAR.

The results shown in Fig.11 show that the most sensitive variables in this project all relate to the operational phase. The forecast of the market volume for the product and the selling price are particularly significant. Timely completion is also of importance. This is frequently the case for cash-earning projects. The

45

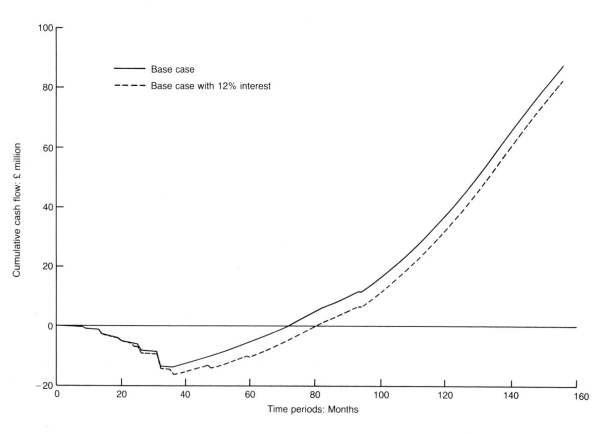

Fig. 10. New Industrial Plant project: cumulative cash flow graph

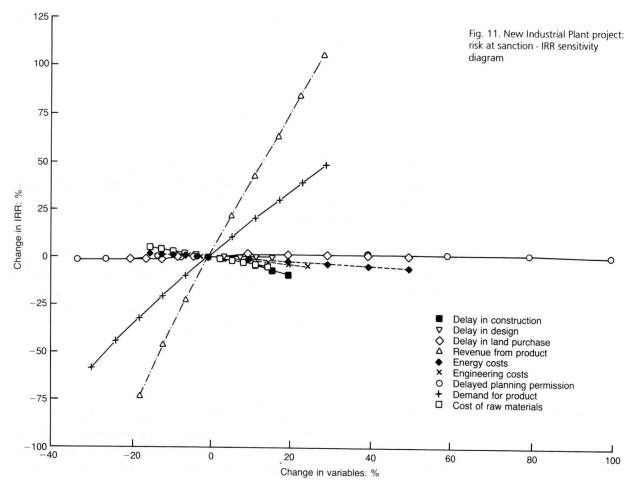

Fig. 11. New Industrial Plant project: risk at sanction - IRR sensitivity diagram

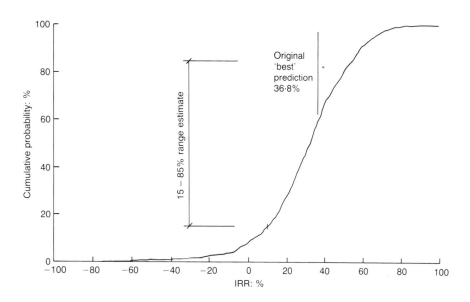

Fig. 12. Risk at sanction - IRR cumulative frequency diagram

viability of such a project entering a competitive consumer market is obviously likely to be greatly dependent on realistic market forecasts and on early commissioning of the facility.

This simple assessment of the individual risks, if carried out early enough, can and should aid management strategy for the project. Additional market surveys may be then initiated to increase confidence in the forecasts and, during the engineering phase, emphasis given to achievement of the programme even at the expense of additional cost [28].

Combined risk

In practice it is likely that some combination of the uncertainties considered individually during sensitivity analysis will be encountered. It is therefore desirable to make some assessment of the implications of the combined risk. This has been done for the above case by assigning probabilities of occurrence to each of the major variables and performing a risk analysis (of the Monte Carlo type). 1000 combinations have been simulated. The results are presented as a cumulative frequency diagram in Fig. 12.

The allocation of probabilities of occurrence to each of the variables included in the risk analysis is subjective. The personnel responsible for the original single-figure estimates should therefore be involved in selecting them. The range and pattern specified for each variable should be based on the degree and nature of uncertainty about the original predictions perceived by the initiator.

Interpretation and perception of risk

The results of the risk analysis as shown in Fig. 12 should be interpreted as giving a guide to the likely out-turn of the project. The original single figure prediction of 36.8% is now seen to have been optimistic, as there is a 60% probability that the IRR will be less than this value. A range estimate of IRR should be substituted. In this example stating a mean IRR of 32% and a 15-85% range of 10-55% would

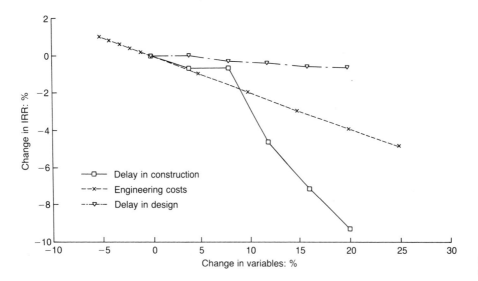

Fig. 13. Design and construction risks: sensitivity diagram

be more meaningful, i.e. there is an 85% probability of achieving an IRR of less than 55%, and only a 15% probability of the IRR falling below 10%.

It must also be accepted that not all risks are included. The exclusions should be stated. For instance, only a small range of operating efficiency has been considered for this plant, but in the extreme case that the plant failed to produce an acceptable product, even for only a short period, the market could be irretrievably affected.

Study of the relative sensitivity of variables on a common scale, as in Fig.11, is valuable and, as mentioned above, will aid definition of the project management policy. It is however also necessary to consider, 'think through' and understand the implications of the individual risks and uncertainties.

Sensitivities of the IRR to variables in the engineering phase of the project are shown in Fig.13. As indicated in Fig.13, delay in completing construction becomes critical immediately the one month of float is consumed. The time-related nature of engineering costs is clear, but the diagram is likely to give a misconception of the effect of delay in design as this appears to have little effect, whereas on reflection it is obvious that it may produce a knock-on effect on construction and therefore timely commissioning. In this project there is float in the design activities, as the critical path in Fig.9 passes through 'Planning permission' and 'Land purchase.' In the sensitivity display in Fig.13 the range of variation plotted for 'Design' is too small to show the full implications of delay. Design delay can affect construction, so the two should be correlated.

Risk at different project stages

The risk spectrum usually reduces as a project proceeds, as activities are completed and confidence is gained in market predictions.

The likely change in risk to the IRR between the sanctioning and commissioning of New Industrial Plant is illustrated in Fig.14, and quantified in Table 4.

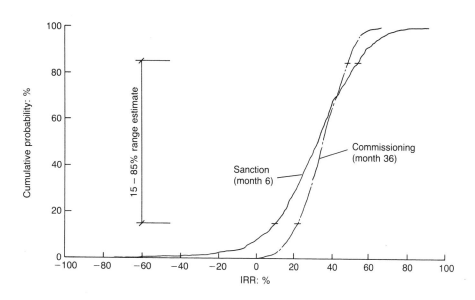

Fig. 14. Change in cumulative risk from sanctioning stage to commissioning

The results shown in Fig.14 and Table 4 have been obtained assuming that the engineering of the project was completed according to plan. Despite this, and the inclusion of updated market forecasts, considerable risk remains for the client at the start of the operational period. The outlook is, however, much brighter !

For any risky project the analysis should be therefore revised at regular intervals during implementation. If up-to-date forecasts are provided by those responsible for the original estimate, this is an excellent form of personal accountability and feedback. Reappraisal should also ensure that project management continue to work to realistic targets.

Financial criteria

We should emphasize that a variety of financial criteria should normally be used to quantify projects for any comparisons, not just IRR as in the example. It should also be noted that using only the mean values of IRR could lead to underestimation of the residual risk.

Reference

84. J. G. Perry and P. A. Thompson. Construction finance and cost escalation. *Proc. Instn Civ. Engrs*, Part 1, 1977, **62**, Nov., 623-643.

Table 4. Change in cumulative risk from sanctioning stage to commissioning

Prediction	IRR %		
		Probability range	
		15%	85%
Basic 'best estimate' (excluding risk)	36.77		
At sanction	31.96 (mean)	10	55
At commissioning	36.11 (mean)	22	48

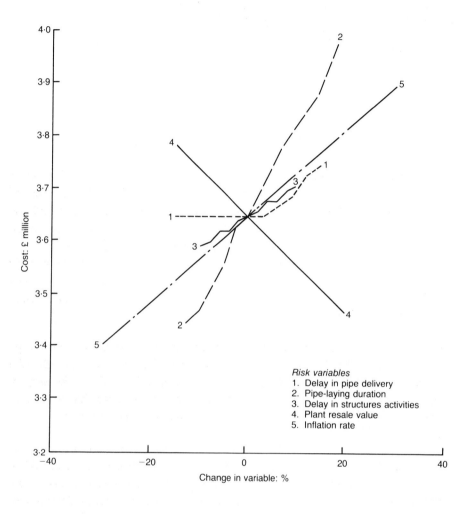

Fig. 15. Overseas pipeline sensitivity diagram

Appendix B: Tenders - quantifying risk to contractors

Probability analysis provides a method for a contractor to quantify the risk he will carry [80]. For example, for a contract for the construction of 100 km of pipeline in the Middle East the contractor was required to import all the construction plant. The consequence of the relatively short construction period was that a large amount of plant was needed. The working life of the plant was expected to exceed the contract duration and so command a considerable resale price. The implications of the major risks perceived by the contractor are shown in Fig.15. All five factors shown produce a significant variation in the estimated basic cost of £3.65m.

Cost is closely related to the time for which resources are employed on this type of work, a fact which is well illustrated in Fig.16. In this diagram the results of a probability analysis are plotted to give contours which define the likely range of outcome of the contract. It is apparent that there is a greater chance of both contract cost and contract duration increasing rather than decreasing.

The diagram also shows that there is only a 40% probability of the final cost falling within the range £3.58m to £3.78m, and a 70% probability that it will be between £3.49m and £3.85m. The contractor's problem is to make adequate provision for these risks and at the same time to submit a competitive tender which is likely to win the job.

The significance of the residual risk arising from plant resale and inflation is apparent from Fig.17. This shows how the spectrum of risk reduces during the course of the contract.

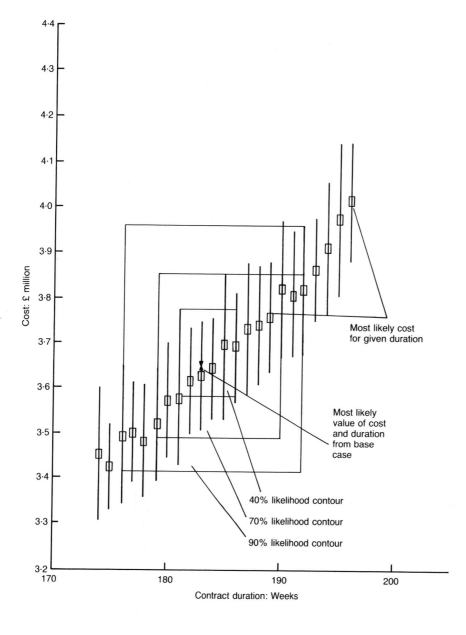

Fig. 16. Overseas pipeline cost and time graph. The cost ranges indicate the values which lie within ± 1 standard deviation of the most likely cost for each given duration

53

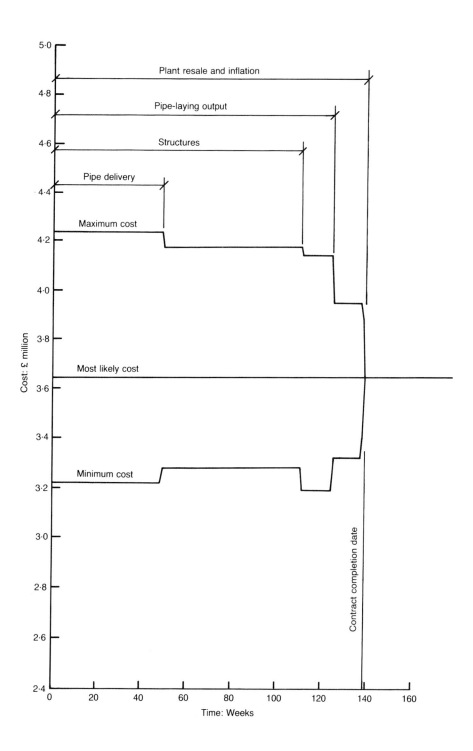

Fig. 17. Overseas pipeline cost
ranges from probability analysis

Appendix C: Bibliography

54

R. S. Anderson *et al. Risk analysis in offshore development projects.* SINTEF, Safety and Reliability Department, Trondheim, 1983.

J. Bartlett. Business risk in major IT projects. *Project*, 1982, May, 18-21.

L. E. Bussey. *The economic analysis of industrial projects.* Prentice-Hall, New Jersey, 1978.

Construction contract policy: improved procedures and practice. Centre for construction law and management, King's College, London, 1989.

G. C. A. Dickson. Looking risk in the face. *Prof. Engng*, 1988, Sept., 33-35, 78.

J. E. Diekmann. Risk analysis: lessons from artificial intelligence. *Int J. Project Manage.*, 1992, **10**, May, 75-80.

Institution of Professional Engineers, New Zealand. *Engineering risk*, 1983.

W. F. Frantz. Systematic risk management impacts hybrid system projects. *Proc. Project Management Institute symposium.* Calgary, 1990, 275-286.

C. Gregory. *Decision analysis.* Pitman, London, 1988.

P. W. Hetland and I. Jordanger. A humanized approach to intelligent risk management. *Proc. 10th Internet world congress.* Vienna, 1990.

O. Husby and N. J. Smith. Assessing project management software for time and cost control. *Proc. Internet - Nordnet - ICEC congress.* Trondheim, 1991, 129-137.

P. H. McGowan *et al. Allocation and evaluation of risk in construction contracts.* Chartered Institute of Building, 1992, occasional paper no. 52.

Risk analysis: APM seminar report. *The Bulletin*, 1989, June, 11-12, 14.

L. E. Smith *et al.* Improving public works project management using project schedule risk analysis. *Proc. Project Management Institute symposium.* Dallas, 1991, 287-296.

S. H. Wearne. Contract administration and project risks. *Int. J. Project Manage.*, 1992, **10**, Feb., 39-41.

D. G. Woodward et al. BOOT update - the model concession agreement and financing issues. *Project*, 1991, Nov., 23-26.

Appendix D: Research team

1983-86
Project Management Group: The University of Manchester Institute of Science
& Technology

Supervisors
Professor Peter Thompson
Dr John Perry

Research assistants (full-time)
Mr Ross Hayes
Dr Gillian Willmer

Part-time
Mr Paul Jobling
Mr Tom Nicholson

1989-91
Project Management Group: The University of Manchester Institute of Science
& Technology

Supervisor
Professor Peter Thompson

Research assistant (full-time)
Miss Catriona Norris

Part-time
Dr Stephen Wearne
School of Civil Engineering: The University of Birmingham

Supervisor
Professor John Perry

Research assistants (full-time)
Dr Cormac McCarthy
Mr Luke Mulekezi